T0129700

Try On Your Own Shoes

James Roberson

WESTBOW
P R E S S®
A DIVISION OF THOMAS NELSON
& ZONDERVAN

WestBow Press books may be ordered through booksellers or by contacting:

WestBow Press
A Division of Thomas Nelson & Zondervan
1663 Liberty Drive
Bloomington, IN 47403
www.westbowpress.com
1 (866) 928-1240

ISBN: 978-1-9736-8776-4 (sc)
ISBN: 978-1-9736-8778-8 (hc)
ISBN: 978-1-9736-8777-1 (e)

Library of Congress Control Number: 2020904734

Print information available on the last page.

WestBow Press rev. date: 4/3/2020

CONTENTS

INTRODUCTION: IT IS TIME TO BE *YOURSELF*

That can be a struggle in this hour we are living in. The world is full of division and stereotypes. If someone were to ask you to define who you truly are, what would your answer be? Would numerous thoughts of others' opinions of you come to the surface and you pick which to speak as your identity? Would you let a situation you've faced become your answer to define you, or would you look at the color of your skin to determine your answer? My purpose for this book is to help individuals find out who they are, so that instead of living a life comparing themselves to others, they can be secure in their identities.

I want you to understand that you no longer have to measure who you are by what you have. I want to help people stop putting themselves on a popularity scale, weighing themselves and their self-worth by the standards of the world's approval. We must know that no one has to chase money, believing that their identity is determined by the riches they possess. I know many of us grew up saying, "I just want to be rich when I get older," so we chase money, not knowing that what God has placed in us can produce what we need.

It was a journey for me to find my purpose and to discover who I am. My story, which later became a testimony, is what inspired me to write this book. I went from being a soldier in the US military to being a veteran at a young age. I was diagnosed with multiple sclerosis at the age of nineteen. This is an unfortunate health condition that devastated me. I went through the stages of "why me?" and being upset that my life seemed to be changing for the worst. The condition made me legally blind, and through me losing my sight, the Lord helped me to truly see who I am. Jesus is a healer, and I do not want you to doubt that. Through becoming legally blind, my eyes were opened to see from his view. God has truly changed my life and helped me to see who I really am in Christ. I want this book to set your eyes on discovering who you truly are.

Focus on what the Word of God says about you and not what people's opinions say about you. In the Bible it says, "before I formed you in the womb, I knew you" (Jeremiah 1:5 NIV). Right there, this lets us know, it is God who knew us before anyone else. Just meditate on that. I struggled with believing a lot of opinions growing up, so when I came in contact with God's thoughts about me, it blew my mind, and it was hard to receive at first.

The potential that God has placed in you may seem uncommon according to the opinions that have been said about you.

The time has come for you to discover yourself, to know your identity, and to be able to discern what's not your identity. Let us open our hearts and our minds and be ready to receive. I thank God for you, and I pray you receive what the Lord has to say through the words he led me to write and that it blesses your life abundantly!

CHAPTER 1

It Is Not External Shoes

Prayer

> Father, I thank you now for your Word. God, open our eyes to see ourselves the way you see us. God, you said before we were formed in the belly that you knew us. Help us to know that person. Renew our hearts, and transform our minds to walk in our true identities. We want to believe and trust in you, Lord. You knitted our inward parts. Show us more of how you created us, Lord, so we can walk in it and not be tossed to and fro with every opinion that's not of you. In Jesus's name, amen.

When you think of something external, you understand that it's outside you. When you think of the word *identity,* you think of being, where your character comes from, and who you are. So putting the words *external identity* together, that's something outside you that defines who you are. The problem with this is that external things aren't promised to stay. If an external thing that once defined you leaves, does that mean who you are has left also? Let me explain. We have to be honest. Some people, unfortunately, didn't grow up with the best clothes or shoes or in the best neighborhoods. Some people did grow up with a lot of material things and did not experience much lack. Whether you were born with a silver spoon in your mouth or not, that does not determine who you are or who you will become. In life, material things can be lost or gained. Your identity, however, should never change unless you have an external identity. If you did not grow up with much or even if you did have plenty, neither determines who you are or what your destiny is.

Your identity is important because it's your foundation, and who you are fuels what you believe you will become. Your identity determines how you see your potential. Many of us are identified by our skin color or even by the environment we grew up in. Both of these things have statistics in the world. Depending on your race, people may try to determine what your outcome in life will be. The environment you grew up in has received statistics of what people who live there will become, but understand that a statistic is not a truth. Just because you grew up in a bad neighborhood, it doesn't mean you have to be poor, a drug dealer, or in a gang. But because we sometimes can receive that statistic, we let our environment grab our faith. So now we believe that our greatest potential is to be in a gang because that's what the neighborhood is full of.

Don't focus on what society says about you. Here's what God

has to say: "Beloved, I pray that you prosper in all things and be in health, just as your soul prospers" (3 John 1:2 NKJV). Do you believe God wants you to prosper? There is much more to say when it comes to what God said about you, and we will go in depth with this throughout the book. You don't look externally to determine who you are or what you will become; you look to God to determine that. External opinions can't define you. You have to speak that and know that. We have to embrace what God has said about us and place our faith in it.

It is important to God that you know your identity. I'll prove that to you through scripture. Some of us have made our identities work, which is still external, but God gave us identity before work, and he did it for a reason. God says, "Let us make man in our image, after our likeness, and let them have dominion over the fish of the sea, and over the fowl of the air, and over the cattle, and over all the earth, and over every creeping thing that creeps upon the earth" (Genesis 1:26 KJV). The following chapter says, "The Lord God took the man and put him in the Garden of Eden to work and take care of it" (Genesis 2:15 NIV). Adam received his identity first, and then God put the man in the garden to work. Work is second because when you know who you are, you can work to your full potential.

Stop and think. Did you set your life like this, or did you put work first to determine your identity? You were never meant to chase your identity or create it, but only to discover it. Know your identity is in God and never external. If you be you, I promise you can do you. But you can't do you while being something or somebody else.

Now knowing these things about external identity, why do we choose them? Why do we make work or our environment our identity? Many people look for external things to make them feel good because internally they have voids. Do you have a void? If so, how do you fill it? The struggle with a lack of confidence or low self-esteem are examples of voids existing within some people. We must understand that a void is just a hunger. The part that hurts us the most is not the void but how we fill it. Sometimes we can fill it with what seems popular, and other times we can fill certain voids with things that are familiar. But is it the correct void filler? It's like we are a puzzle, and a void is an indicator of a piece missing. Some of us have tried to fit a wrong piece into a puzzle. Some of us have dealt with an acceptance void because of being rejected. What can happen later is you grab pride, which seems like a protector but turns into a destroyer of character. Pride is nothing more than a protector from vulnerability, but it also protects from healing. It's sad that so many of us have dealt with this, but God can heal it all. We have to heal.

There are cases where if you don't know how to love yourself internally, you begin to look for people to love you. When you're not satisfied with who you are, you start to go along with others to get along, afraid of rejection because rejection will expose the void of lack of love and acceptance. That's how people get hurt in relationships, and the ones outside looking in don't understand why they keep going back. They have made people their void filler for love, and they have met someone who has said "I love you," so they run to that person, afraid that if they leave, they won't have love.

I really want you to know who you are and to understand

the God who created you is the only one who can permanently fill voids—not something that can leave any moment. Nothing external can define you, because it's temporary. Nobody defines you, only God. This includes any illness some may be battling with. A sickness is still external. If you have been diagnosed with a sickness or disease, don't put on the shoes of that sickness, because it is not who God called you. Your name is not that illness, and you shouldn't take on its character. You were made in the image of God, not the image of sickness. When you introduce yourself, you're not introducing cancer or diabetes. This is important because you need to see illness like God sees it, instead of how the world sees it. Instead of speaking depression, cancer, MS, or lupus over yourself, begin to speak and believe healing over your life. When you allow yourself to put your identity to something external, you are putting trust in that and not God. Your character becomes it. You begin to conform to it.

You will always know if someone really knows who they are. If their identity is in money, their mood will change depending on how much money they possess. If they've conformed to people, they begin to change themselves according to who they are around. God looks internally to define you. You should value what's in you. The Bible says, "Love your neighbor as yourself" (Matthew 23:39 NIV). When you're walking in your true identity, you can have good relationships because you're not hoping that they can fill what you're supposed to already have filled. Your mentality is like Christ, and you love like Christ. Your voids are filled through God and not external things, so who you are is never defined by what you have or what you do.

Testimony:
My External Identity

The thing I would cleave to was working out. Growing up, confidence wasn't really my strong suit. That was, until high school, when I started exercising. I'm sure we all have had that thing we were just so good at doing. Well, this was mine. In high school, I wasn't the best at sports, but when it came to the gym, I could easily go into it with a confident smile. For you, it could be something different. You might be a good athlete or the best at your job. Often we can cleave to that thing we're gifted at. When someone says the name *Michael Jordan,* the thought that comes to mind is basketball. When you say the name *Tom Brady,* football comes up. Well for me, it was weightlifting. When people, or even I myself, thought of my name, weightlifting was often attached to it.

What I was doing was a good thing, but since I made it my identity, it was not a God thing. There is nothing wrong with weightlifting or sports, but remember those things never told you, "Never will I leave you; never will I forsake you" (Hebrews 13:5 NIV). They can't say it because they are temporary. For me, growing up not knowing my identity in Christ led to seeking fitness titles to identify myself. I wanted my gift to talk for me and define me. I had to perform constantly and work to keep my identity when it came to weightlifting. Someone else might need work and money or clothes to keep his or her identity. A title is about doing works that do not help you reach your full potential, but when your identity is in Christ, it is about being who you were called to be, reaching fulfillment. I struggled for years doing works for a title or certain image for others to perceive me. I walked around cleaving to working out as my identity, but out of nowhere, I got diagnosed with MS. I was upset and angry because of the disease but more so not being able to work out any longer like I used to. I put my identity in working out, and when that decreased, I thought I had decreased. I knew I was getting weaker; my ability to do certain things was decreasing, and so was my confidence. That is what happens when you put the creation above the Creator. Now, listen: working out is cool. I still do it. But now I know that's not my identity. My identity is in Christ. So no matter what leaves me, I'm forever secure in who I am.

A job is cool, people are cool, working out, sports are all good things. I'm not pulling you away from them. What I am saying is, be secure in who you are. The Bible says, "heaven and earth shall pass away, but my word shall not pass away" (Matthew 24:35 KJV). If your identity is in something that can leave, that's not it. I don't care who or what said *I won't leave you.* If it's a creation, don't put your identity in it. Stand on the Word of God, and know who you are in Christ.

Prayer for Chapter 2

Father, I thank you now for who you are. I thank you for my parents. Help me, Lord, to always honor them. You said you know the plans you have for me, plans to prosper me and not to harm me. Plans of an expected end. God, teach me the path you have for me. Help me to be who you created me to be. I want to build a personal relationship with you for myself, not through my parents' relationship with you. I desire to know you on a more intimate level, Lord. In Jesus's name I pray, amen.

CHAPTER 2

You Are Not Your Parents

I want to begin with an example in the Bible of how people saw Jesus and how they mixed him up with who his parents were. The passage reads, "and they said, is not this Jesus the son of Joseph, whose father and mother we know? How is it then that he saith, 'I came down from heaven?'" (John 6:42 KJV). In this story, never did they say that Mary and Joseph were bad parents. But they couldn't agree with Jesus's statement because of who his parents were, the statement, "I came down from heaven." This was not something Jesus's parents said or talked about, so when Jesus said this statement, the people were confused and put Jesus's identity as the same as his parents'.

I want to talk to someone who feels that people have tried to attach who you are or who you will become with who your parents are. Have you been misunderstood because the direction God is taking your life isn't the same direction your parents took? Can you relate? People tell you, "You're going to be just like your mom or dad." Now, I'm not saying that's a bad thing, but God has given everyone a purpose, and the purpose your parents have been given may not be the same purpose God has for you. God might have two different plans for the child and for the parents. Never allow anyone to say who you will become based on who your parents are. I say this because we have all made mistakes. Sometimes parents make mistakes, and this might have had a bad effect on their lives. An awesome man of God once said, "Sometimes people will put a period on your life like it's over for you." No one should put a period over anyone's life. The mistake of the parent doesn't define the future of the child. We have to be in a place to understand that God is the only one who holds the key to our future.

The Bible says, "many are the plans in a person's heart, but it is the LORD'S purpose that prevails" (Proverbs 19:21 NIV). You might have grown up walking in other plans, but it doesn't change who God has originally called you to be. Your identity in Christ never changes, but the person who needs to know that more than anyone else is you. One thing that hinders this, which is common, is unforgiveness. There are many of us who have taken unforgiveness lightly. You might have gone through something as a child and bottled it up like it doesn't matter. For instance, your dad walked out of your life, and you might say it didn't affect you, but truthfully it probably did. One thing that will set us free from it all is forgiveness. Unforgiveness can bring a weight on your life. Unforgiveness can change your perception of life and cause you to see things according to the bad that has happened in life. It can cause you to see through bitterness. Dad never said he loved you, so now you look at men bitterly. You've tainted your own perspective because you feel like now you can't be loved, like you can't be accepted. There is importance to forgiving. Instead of being scared to be vulnerable and trying to cover the hurt with pride or nice external things, free yourself from the pain, so that the process of healing can manifest.

Many times, healing cannot begin because we want to wait until the person who caused the pain apologizes. When you do that, you put the key to unlocking your healing in the palm of that person's hands. It is not healthy or wise to continue to be hurt internally until they come and say those words. Do not allow what happened in your childhood to leave you stuck. The Bible says "when I was a child, I spake as a child, I understood as a child, but when I became a man, I put away childish things" (1 Corinthians 13:11 KJV). You grow up physically as an adult, but your mind can get stuck at a certain place from your childhood. It's time to start fresh and forgive. Be who God has called you to be, and let nothing hold you back. You may not have felt accepted as a kid, but you are accepted in Christ Jesus. You may not have felt peace as a kid, but Jesus is the prince of peace. You may not have felt love as a kid, but God is love. As you walk in who you are in Christ, know that we are created in the image and likeness of God. We must then understand that love is a part of our identity. When you know who you are in Christ, you'll know what true love really is and walk in it. So let's open ourselves up. Let God heal those wounds. Love your parents, and most importantly love yourself. Know that God has validated you and loves you. I want us to love ourselves; don't let your future be dictated according to your past.

Now, with everything that I have said, let me show you, through the Word of God, how you should look at your parents. I'm going to use our example, Jesus Christ and his life as a young man with his parents. In the Bible it says, "'Why were you searching for me? Didn't you know I had to be in my Father's house?' But they did not understand what he was saying to them. Then he went down to Nazareth with them and was obedient to them. But his mother treasured all these things in her heart" (Luke 2:49–51 NIV). The Word also says, "children, obey your parents in all things: for this is well pleasing in the sight of the Lord" (Colossians 3:20 NIV). Your purpose and calling in life may be different from your parents' and maybe even misunderstood by them, but that doesn't give you permission to disrespect or dishonor them. Despite anything, love, respect, and honor them.

Your parents can help you reach the place of your potential in God. A powerful scripture says, "Not only so, but we glory in tribulation also: knowing that tribulation works patience; and patience, experience; experience, hope" (Romans 5:3–4 KJV). Situations produce something. The situations that your parents have been through have produced experience. The experience taught them something and has produced counsel. That counsel that they learn from their experience can teach you something. I would never tell you not to listen to your parents, because they do want to teach you something. Be careful not to look down on your parents for what they went through, because you could end up going through the exact same thing if you don't listen to them. God has a purpose for you, and it might not be the same as your parents', but there are things that all parents can teach their children. Things like honesty, discipline, the Word of God, and other key tools that will help you succeed in life. Love your parents, listen to them, understand them, and observe their lives. Always remember this if nothing else: we do not love based off of how people love us, but we always love based off of how God loves us. So when we love, we don't look at people, we look at God. This leads to the next chapter, because you can only know how God loves by knowing him.

Testimony: My Parents and I

My mom is very passionate about the medical field. She has been working in that field for a long time and coaching/helping the family when medical issues happen in their lives. I, on the other hand, don't understand how someone could give a person an injection. No matter how passionate my mom was about her work, she never imposed her passion on me. Instead, she would be hard on me about things that would help discipline me and give me a strong character for my passion. I was not a perfect kid, but I do remember the things my mom taught me, and I'm greatly appreciative for it. My dad is a general manager at a restaurant and has been for several years. He has a strong character and boldness in him. He is a good guy. Both of my parents are hard workers. My mom raised me, and the things I shared about my dad are what I've learned about him from the times we've connected and talked. I love them both. I honor them and thank God for them both. When I was a kid, though, my dad wasn't really in my life. I was around four years old when he and Mom split up. My father and I would go years without speaking or seeing one another. Growing up without my father caused me to seek validation from wrong things and have the wrong perception of what a man is. I thought toughness was one thing that validated you to be a man. I thought weakness and tears took away manhood in a sense. One thing I did that would hurt me was taking things literally. If something was said to me, and I received it, I soaked it up like a sponge. So growing up, when people said that tears, expressing feelings, and being vulnerable were signs of weakness, I tried really hard to keep things in. If my dad and I would talk and he would disappoint me, I would immediately try to conceal it. Even if other adults, including my mom, made me promises and let me down, I would conceal the hurt.

Eventually, living like that, I started building less and less of an expectation. I had very little trust and very little expectation. I didn't want anybody to try to make me believe them, because if I did, I would agree to be vulnerable to them. Living this way hurt me badly, because when Jesus came into my life, I didn't know how I was supposed to trust his promises since I'd had little belief in promises before. I had built my heart this way so I wouldn't get hurt. Not only did I struggle in believing people's promises but affection, connection, and intimacy as well. I didn't know how to connect well because I didn't know how to be vulnerable. I was dealing with rejection, resentment, and anger that I had concealed for so long. I just thought it was who I was. All I knew was that I started to take every little disappointment as rejection. If someone picked anyone else over me or told me no, I didn't know how to express the hurt, and I would just shut down. I now know I was seeking validation. I was seeking to be around someone I could learn from, someone who could teach me how to release the pain of rejection, accept me at my weak point, and someone I felt comfortable being vulnerable around.

The Bible says "Lo, this only have I found, that God hath made man upright; but they have sought out many inventions" (Ecclesiastes 7:29 KJV). If people don't know how they were created, they go seeking validation from wrong places. When the home doesn't validate the child, understand that influence is everywhere. When a child longs for acceptance, he or she will find it somewhere. People yearn for acceptance and validation, including children. We need it. With my acceptance problem, I took failure very hard. Sports were a big example. I didn't want to disappoint my coaches, but it always seemed like something was going wrong. I began to take on a perfectionist spirit. I began to get scared to start, because if I started and others didn't accept my finished work, it would crush my self-esteem. In relationships, it was the same thing. If I opened up to someone who looked like they were nice, seemed like they wanted my best interest, I'd do anything for them. A lack of validation makes a lack of discernment.

It is very important for children's parents to be active in their lives. Let them receive love from you first. Let that love be the God kind of love. Let them receive their influence from you first, a godly influence. I believe the home should be the foundation where children get their validation, affirmation, and influence from first. I'm not a parent yet, but I observe. Let's restore the connection between the parent and child. Let's get right. Let's stop this cycle of the father being absent from the home. It's horrible to feel like it's common for a dad not to be there. I believe when the homes are set in order according to the will of God, it can heal the identity crisis that we face today. We can't do this on our own. We can't restore families on our own. We need God because we can't do it without him. We need him, so let's make sure we know him.

Prayer for Chapter 3

Father, I thank you now for being an on-time God. The Earth is the Lord's in the fullness thereof. God, you are the beginning and the end, the first and the last. We acknowledge you as the Creator. Create in me a yearning to know you, God. You said I was created in your image, according to your Word. If I'm going to know myself, I must know you. Teach me your ways. Create in me a hunger for you, Lord. In Jesus's name I pray, amen.

CHAPTER 3

Know Your Source

I n a relationship, do you go after the person's heart, or do you
go after his or her hand? When you go after the person's hand,
you can't say that you really know them, but you are familiar
with the person's benefits. You really don't know if they love you
or not; you don't even know if you love them or not, but you love
what they can do for you. That relationship is not a very good
one, but sadly it does happen. Now, the other relationship, when
you are after the person's heart, this relationship is intimate.
When you know someone's heart, you know them.

The Bible says, "For as he thinketh in his heart, so is he:
Eat and drink, saith he to thee; but his heart is not with thee"
(Proverbs 23:7 KJV). This is letting us know that when you know
a person's heart, you know them. Well, let's flip it to us and God.
How many of us know God? Are we after his hand or his heart?
Why is this relevant to your identity? In Genesis 1:26 AMP, the
Word tells us that man was created in the Lord's image and in

his likeness. In order to know you, you have to know God, and to know God, you have to know his heart. It's awesome when we are blessed with a nice new car or a new house. Remember, those are external things. How are you inwardly? You are familiar with God's hand, but what about God's heart? You know God when you know his heart. Sometimes without knowing, we pray to God for things that we have a deeper relationship with than him, which is idolatry. Remember that your potential is inside your identity. Whatever you say or believe you are, you put your potential in it. We should want to operate in the fullness of how we were created.

The Bible says, "now unto him that is able to do exceeding abundantly above all that we ask or think, according to the power that works within us" (Ephesians 3:20 KJV). In order for us to embrace our potential, we have to embrace ourselves. In order to embrace ourselves, we have to embrace God. We have to get to know him. God has a purpose for all of us. A preacher once said, "Know that whatever you were born to do, you were built to do it." Well, one common problem is that we desire to do what we were born to do, but we question if we are truly able to do it. Moses had an issue with this and is great a example of what happens when purpose is revealed but you are not secure in or don't know who you are.

Let's take a look at the conversation between Moses and God about his true identity and purpose being revealed. The Bible says, "So now, go. I am sending you to Pharaoh to bring my people the Israelites out of Egypt. But Moses said to God, 'Who am I that I should go to Pharaoh and bring the Israelites out of Egypt?'" (Exodus 3:10–11 NIV). Sounds like us? "Who am I to write this book? I've never been good at literature." or "Who am I to pastor a church?" Do not doubt who God has called you, but you have to know you, and to discover you, you have to know God. We can say things like, "I've never been a leader at anything." If God is a leader, that same nature that's in him is in you. Whatever God said about you, that's the truth about you, but we have to know what he said about us. Some of us beat ourselves up about mistakes, and instead of looking at what the Bible says about us when we make mistakes, we let others' opinions consume us. Now we battle with forgiving ourselves, not knowing that God has already forgiven you when you ask him.

We're constantly striving to live up to someone else's expectation, just so they can give us an identity that's not even ours. It's time to really know you. If you deny who Christ is, not only will he deny you to the Father, but you are also denying who you are because you are in him. Let's build a relationship with the Lord and discover who we are in him. Begin to study his Word, find a church, get into a place of prayer, and receive a revelation of who you truly are, because as you begin to seek God, he will begin to show you who you truly are. While you are seeking God, it is important to detach old identities that are not you. Get in a place where your focus can shift and be stayed on God. The Word says, "a double minded man is unstable in all his ways" (James 1:8 KJV). God doesn't want you operating in what another person said about you that's contrary to him. We want God's Word to be your foundation, your first priority, your first love. God wants all of you to discover yourselves and be all that he has called you to be. God will reveal who you are through a process.

Testimony: Me Getting to Know God

Growing up, I didn't go to church very often. I went off and on till I was about seven years old. When I turned fifteen years old, I received an invitation from a friend to attend her church, so I went. I started to attend regularly. This church is the same church where I met my wonderful wife at sixteen years old. Since I was a little older, it was my choice to go. I liked the people at the church. They always seemed nice and in a good mood. Even though I was attending church so often, I still hadn't built a true relationship with God. Fast forward a few years to when I was nineteen years old and diagnosed with MS. I had a lot going on at this time. I had been experiencing symptoms of MS for about a year, and I was diagnosed five months before I turned twenty.

When I started going to church again, I was looking for something or someone to help me through my difficult time. I was aware that I couldn't stay in the military because of MS. I knew my ability to work out like I used to was slowly going downhill because of my physical disadvantages. Working out was the last thing I had to cover my voids. I was hungry for a new void filler. I started attending a church, and the preacher was ministering to me. He didn't know my situation, but he spoke to me as if he did. That encounter woke me up. What really caught my attention was hearing that God has a purpose and a plan for my life. That God has an assignment specifically for my life. Scripture that really began to encourage me was, "be confident in this very thing, that he that hath begun a good work in you shall perform it until the day of Jesus Christ" (Philippians 1:6 KJV). I would hear that God would fulfill his purpose in me and I have potential that God has put in me. I began to want God more and more, but I was still dealing with rejection, lack of confidence, and low self-esteem. I wanted God for the wrong reasons. I wanted what he could do for me more than a real relationship with him. I begin to ask questions and listen closely when it came to purpose. How to find it? How to get to it? How to secure it?

I did this for a couple of years. I was wrong for doing this, because my motive was wrong. I mismanaged priorities being like this. I begin to want the work of the Lord so badly that I would choose it over my wife. I had to learn that you never put the work of the Lord above the Lord of the work. When God is first, your priorities will be in order. When the work of the Lord is first, it will be out of order every time, and though it is the work of the Lord, it's still considered God's hand and not his heart. God had to deal with me inwardly. I needed to sit down and heal. God began to deal with my rejection, taking me on a season of repentance and deliverance. I could have continued to pursue ministry and not God. That's a very scary and dangerous thing to do.

I'm grateful for God's love and mercy that brought me out of that mentality. God had to heal me and deliver me from things of my childhood and properly fill the voids I had. He taught me the true love of God and how identity is who you are and not what you do. He taught me what it means to rest in him and be still. This was very important because when you identify with what you do instead of knowing who you are, you will never rest. My foundation couldn't be the work of the Lord. Most importantly, God taught me his heart, so I could be a good steward of what comes out of his hand. I love him very much. He is very faithful, and I'm grateful he is in my life.

Prayer for Chapter 4

Father, I thank you now for your Word. God, you said to endure like a good soldier. You said that you will gird us up with strength for the battle. God, we submit to your process. We now transform our mind according to your will, and no matter what happens, let us keep our eyes stayed on you. In Jesus's name, amen.

Put Off the Old Man and Put On the New Man

One thing I encourage through this process is to trust God and keep the spiritual eyes on what's to come. I say this because the process is a transition. You are putting your old self behind and putting on the new you. Though it's the true you, it's new to you. It is like surgery. When you think of surgery, things that come to mind are cutting and healing. That's what the process does. It detaches all of the unnecessary things that were blocking what God wants to do, and builds you up into what God wants. Jesus once said, "I know that you are Abraham's descendants. Yet you are looking for a way to kill me because you have no room for my word." (John 8:37 NIV). Jesus was speaking truth. He brought the kingdom of God back. The problem was, when he spoke, the people had no room to receive him because they were filled with other things.

That's also what happened with the children of Israel. God delivered them out of Egypt, and Egypt was bondage. They were treated badly and were forced to perform hard labor daily as a way to make them obey and submit to Pharaoh. God brought them out of Egypt to dwell in the Promised Land, flowing with milk and honey. To transition from bondage and hard labor to that awesome land seemed like an easy transition outside looking in, but the children of Israel struggled with it. The issue was, they were in Egypt a long time, and their mentality conformed to that culture and environment. They made bondage their normal, and they adapted to it. When they left Egypt to go to the Promised Land, every time something went wrong, they missed Egypt. They missed bondage.

Sound crazy? Well, let's bring it to us. Some of us may have had voids. We could be dealing with rejection, fear, loneliness, and lack of love. We might have used things like people, pride, food, money, and jobs to fill those voids. Though they might have fulfilled us temporarily and not permanently, we adapted to it and made it our normal. We got used to it, and we used them to protect us from feeling the pain of those voids. Trust was formed in those void fillers, and whenever trust is formed, you give it a piece of yourself. Just like a trust fall, you trust those fillers to catch you by filling those present voids. When something has a piece of you, detaching from it is not easy. I am not saying don't trust, but know what to trust. Trust God. That's why God needs room in your heart. Remember, whoever has your heart has you. The Lord wants all of us, and he will convert you as you submit to his process.

This is not easy because you are reprogramming yourself by breaking habits and replacing them with the things of God.

Staying encouraged and allowing God to deal with your heart is key. In Psalms, it explains how to build your trust. It says, "Those who know your name trust in you, for you, Lord, have never forsaken those who seek you" (Psalms 9:10 NIV). Our knowledge of Jesus builds our trust in Jesus. One thing that has to be changed through the process is your influence. What your eyes see constantly and what you hear influences you. Your influence determines your direction. So, for example, if your direction is to be a mechanic, you wouldn't really need the influence of a dentist. With your identity, your true identity is in Christ. If the direction you want to go is in Christ, the influence you need is the influence to move you in that direction. Now, some of us can't change our environment at the moment, but you still have the ability to determine what gets in you to influence you.

Realize that everything has a direction. People have a direction, sin has a direction, but the question is, where did God say to go? This will determine what influences you. I know sin is not the most popular topic. The process will cleanse you and help you overcome bad habits that lead to sin. In 2 Corinthians, it speaks on this. It says, "having therefore these promises, dearly beloved, let us cleanse ourselves from all filthiness of the flesh and spirit, perfecting holiness and the fear of God" (2 Corinthians 7:1 KJV). Our identity in Christ has the spirit of Christ; it makes us new creatures. Everyone should strive to be more Christlike. The process prunes sinful habits off of you and brings a stronger conviction to do what is right in the Lord's sight. You want to sow into your heart what you want to reap in your life. Spend more time studying the Word of God, developing a prayer life, meditating on Jesus, praising and worshiping, and growing that intimacy with God. All of these things will change your circle, so your company will change as your love for Jesus grows.

Now, of course, the enemy will try to distract you. He will try to move your focus because you're coming into the true you. Your eyes will begin to open, and you'll be able to walk in what God said about you. For example, all of these racial issues that are going on around the world, they're looking at the skin color and seeing it in the flesh. They say a black person did it or a white cop did it, and none of it is true. The Bible says, "For we wrestle not against flesh and blood, but against principalities, against powers, against the rulers of the darkness of this world, against spiritual wickedness in high places" (Ephesians 6:12 KJV). It is a spiritual warfare, not the flesh. Some of us fight the flesh, not knowing that it's a spirit working in the person.

You'll know how to handle it properly as you continue your walk with God and grow spiritually. Christ says this about your true identity: "I have given you authority to trample on snakes and scorpions and to overcome all the power of the enemy; nothing will harm you" (Luke 10:19 NIV). Your true identity has power over the enemy. It's not a flesh-and-blood issue like everyone thinks. All types of issues happen in the world, but it's a spirit that's using the person to do the act. The person just does not understand that they're being used by the enemy to do sinful acts. Your true identity in Christ will open your eyes in the spirit; it's the trick of the enemy to see the issue in the flesh. I want us to keep focus on those things that it may push us, encourage us in the Lord. The biggest thing I believe that hinders us in the process is distractions and becoming weary. There is good news, because God has assigned someone on Earth to you who can help you develop what God has put in you, that you may become all he has called you to be. Someone who can hold you accountable, pour wisdom into you, and encourage you. I encourage all of us through the process to keep going, stay focused, and submit to God. This process is a becoming process. Daily we strive to become more like Christ and strong in spirit. Let's leave room for God to be God in our lives and do his work in us. I know that it's all going to work together for our good. We just have to trust God through it all!

Testimony: My Process

The two things that were really attached to me were working out and people. It's not that either of those things is bad, but honestly, I will say that working out was an idol to me, and people were my way of filling my acceptance void. The process I went through taught me to put God first. When I was diagnosed with MS, that's when things started changing for me. I was stubborn. I wasn't grateful for the process then, but I am grateful now because I understand the purpose of it. I couldn't work out like I used to, so my excitement for it decreased. At first I took it hard. Whenever something becomes an idol, it's definitely something that means a lot to you and has a strong influence on who you are. As the ability to work out decreased, it was detaching from me. Without my ability to work out the way I used to and having the physique I was accustomed to, my confidence with people decreased as well. I felt unaccepted, unlike myself, and angry. My voids were exposed, and my void fillers couldn't help me. When it came to God, I was becoming open to receive him in my life. King David in the Bible explains something that relates to the process. He says, "My sacrifice, O God, is a broken spirit; a broken and contrite heart you, God, will not despise" (Psalms 51:17 NIV). I had no room for God, and my heart wasn't in the right place to receive him at first.

Being diagnosed with MS didn't feel good at all, but it did open me up to God. I found out I was getting out of the army at age nineteen as medically retired, yet I had planned to do twenty years. I didn't really talk much, so I was distant with people. The only person I really talked to was my wife, but even she knew I had changed, looking at my demeanor. I just couldn't wrap my mind around what was happening. Most of us always want an explanation why certain things happen to us. I didn't understand at that moment, but God did intervene in my life. He is always on time. My wife went to church consistently; I, on the other hand, didn't care for going at the time. I would go just to say I went.

We visited a church, and I didn't understand then, but God began to speak to me through the man of God. He was preaching about husbands and talking about situations and circumstances. God was showing me myself through the sermon. He exposed my selfishness toward my wife. He began to preach on why situations happen. I half-rejected it, yet I wanted to know more. I did decide to go back to the church. No one was able to really get through to me since being diagnosed with MS, so I was curious. More and more, the man of a God would say something, and it would draw me. It kept happening Sunday after Sunday, Bible study after Bible study. I eventually got an urge to study the Word for myself. My influences slowly began to change. I began to want to know more about God. My perspectives of things began to change. Scriptures like, "But he said to me, My grace is sufficient for you, for my power is made perfect in weakness. Therefore I will boast all the more gladly about my weaknesses, so that Christ's power may rest on me" (2 Corinthians 12:9 NIV). Another scripture that helped me was, "Not only so, but we also glory in our suffering, because we know that suffering produces perseverance; perseverance, character; and character, hope" (Romans 5:3–4 NIV).

These scriptures began to encourage me. They began to strengthen me. My curiosity for Jesus began to increase.

God began to put me in certain atmospheres, be it medical appointments, barbershops, or Wal-Mart, where people wanted to talk about the gospel. The Bible says, "Those who know your name trust in you, for you, Lord, have never forsaken those who seek you" (Psalms 9:10 NIV). The more and more I began to learn about Jesus, the more my trust slowly was building in him. Of course, this was a process, and my trust continues to grow every day. I began to love Jesus. I began to trust Jesus and believe in his Word. My perspective changed slowly from what I saw in the natural to what I saw in the spirit.

My view of my wife began to change for the better. I stopped being bitter toward everyone, including God. I want to encourage my readers that everything you're going through or have been through is working for your good. As I began to learn more about Jesus, the Lord sent godly influences into my life. I want to encourage those who think God has left you, because he has not. He will send godly people into your life to help you on your journey to fulfilling your purpose and walking in your identity.

Prayer for Chapter 5

Father, I thank you now for the mentors you have put into our lives. I pray now, Lord, that they push and empower us to be where you want us to be. Help us all remember that this isn't about us or them, but it's all for the glory of you, God. Anoint our ears and hearts to always hear and receive you, Lord, and being open to the vessel or vessels you have used to speak into our lives. In Jesus's name, amen.

CHAPTER 5

Your Mentors-Partners

Throughout the Bible, you don't see the word *mentor*, but you do see a lot of examples of them. To name a few, there were Joshua and Moses, Elisha and Elijah, Naomi and Ruth. As you study their different lives, you see how each mentor interacts with the mentee and how the mentee receives from the mentor. Now, before I really get started on describing a mentor and how to know who is assigned to you, always remember that a mentor does not come to replace God. I know that we are eager to learn and grow spiritually, but sometimes we can unconsciously put our mentor or spiritual leader in the place of God. Sometimes you have mentors who allow it. The mentor shouldn't have a domineering, manipulative spirit. Mentors should not behave as if they are the source. They are only a vessel being used by God to mentor you, grow you, and encourage you. The mentee should honor, respect, and submit to authority. Do not get caught in idolatry when it comes to your mentor. Mentors should hold you accountable, guide you on the path of Christ, and push you in the direction God wants you to go.

There are great men and women of God out there who are awesome mentors. But understand that not everyone is assigned to you. Not everyone is assigned to push and help you get to where God wants you to go. One way to know who God has assigned to you is by looking at this passage of scripture, which gives us an indicator to tell which mentor is for you. The passage says, "When Elizabeth heard Mary's greeting, the baby leaped in her womb, and Elizabeth was filled with the Holy Spirit" (Luke 1:41 NIV). Further down, Elizabeth explains what happened, saying, "As soon as the sound of your greeting reached my ears, the baby in my womb leaped for joy" (Luke 1:44 NIV). What God has put in you, he wants it all to manifest out. That mentor—who can speak to the thing God has put on the inside of you and give you that inner joy—is probably the one who should be mentoring you. You want someone who will push you past your comfort zone, who wants to see you be who God has called you to be. This seems great when talked about, but it's not the easiest thing to walk out. Your potential is on the inside of you, but it's unknown.

Sometimes we want to be around people who will validate us right where we are—someone who is at the same place we are or even younger spiritually. You have to ask yourself, "Can this type of person challenge me?" Probably not. They make you feel comfortable where you are. Very little correction comes forth, because they see exactly the way you see. We need to be challenged. It's not a bad thing to be exposed. The exposure is not to hurt you, but it shows you where you are and gives you room to grow. It leaves you room to be taught. There are some people who do not expose to help you grow but only with the motive to make you look bad. The Word of God is used for teaching, rebuking, correcting, and training in righteousness, as it says in 2 Timothy 3:16 NIV. Your mentor having a godly character is going to do this in love, but you have to be open to listen. Don't look at them through the eyes of your past. That's one of the ways we miss God, by being stuck in our past.

The mentor needs to be patient, and you have to be open. Someone might have yelled at you, called you a failure, or said you wouldn't amount to anything, but that's not true. Sometimes we can be challenged by our mentor, or correction may come, and we start seeing through the eyes of what happened ten years ago. Then we react like we did ten years ago. We have to trust the mentor God put in our lives and put down the wall. That wall is defensive and won't allow anyone to correct you. If you keep that wall up, you actually are shutting the voice of God out of your life. When God is speaking through someone, we don't want to miss him. Talk to your mentor, because they are here to equip you, not look down on you or discourage you in your vulnerable stages.

Now, concerning vulnerability, the love of God should always be shown. However, do not try to have a mentor who wants to carry you. What do I mean? The mentor who wants to do everything for you. The one who doesn't challenge you and who will make compromises for you. If a baby was carried for five years and never given the opportunity to walk, don't expect him to be able to. He was never challenged to walk, so he doesn't know how to. The mentor might know who they are, they might know their purpose, but they should empower you to know who you are and God's purpose for your life. You want them to challenge you to be who God has called you to be, to challenge you to study the Word of God, develop a prayer life, and correct you in wrongdoing. Leaders birth leaders. That's how it should work.

I remember in school, there would be kids who wanted to cheat off someone's work or wanted someone to do their homework all the time. That mentality seemed okay then, but what happens when you're all alone to do your own work? The mentor shouldn't cripple the mentee. The mentor should empower the mentee to eventually become a mentor. That's true leadership, and that's what Jesus did with his disciples. The process with the mentor and mentee is awesome. A mentor is an experienced adviser. Just as I said in the chapter about parents, the mentor has also made mistakes. They will give you godly wisdom and counsel through the Word of God and life experiences. The mentee just has to be open to listen. Both parties have a part to play. Patience is required from both people. You need a listening ear and a hunger for more of Jesus. Your mentor should want to make a disciple out of you and build you and other people up for God's glory.

Testimony: My Mentor(s) Experience

I've made some mistakes choosing mentors and letting certain people speak into my life. I was the type of person who was indecisive. I've done a lot of people pleasing. I wanted to accomplish something so badly and be good at something, just to build my confidence. Well, with all of those voids and strong desires within, I attracted people to me who talked like they wanted to help me. I was broken and didn't know who I was. A man of God once said, "When you're broken, you have no boundaries." I didn't have much discernment. Now, don't get me wrong—I wasn't the type of person who would do something extreme that could put me in jail, but the mentors I encountered were often domineering. They were manipulative and controlling. It's a terrible thing for someone to take advantage of your vulnerability, but I was so naïve and wanted help, I couldn't see clear to discern. The aggressiveness of the mentors pushed what little discernment I had away, and the surety of them always made me feel unsure. God always opened my eyes to things when I got alone. I would always go from going along with them to being silent when they were wrong to asking questions about right and wrong.

When I got there, it was usually time for the relationship to end. When I left the relationships, I was full of regrets, thinking of the time I lost and the people I may have hurt. I'm speaking about my bad experiences that I've had with mentors so that you can have a stronger spiritual discernment. I don't want anyone to take advantage of you, and I thank God, though it hurt, for the experience that produced wisdom in my life. In my life now, there are people I would say who have a godly influence on me. A previous pastor of mine who is the man of God I was talking about who used to speak to me when I was diagnosed with MS, challenged me to stay on track and stay focused. This man of God wasn't a "feel-good" type of preacher, which was great, because I needed to grow. He once said, "You have to learn to fight. If you don't learn to fight battles, you'll always crumble under pressure." This was definitely something I needed to hear because I want to be planted in the Word through situations and circumstances I face and not allow them to break me.

My previous pastor had a heart for people and loved to pour into me. I thank God for all he taught me. Someone else I want to honor who isn't my mentor but my partner and best friend is my wife. She has been with me at my worst state. She's seen me smile and cry. She doesn't just tell me things where I can say, "You're my wife, and you're supposed to say that." She pushes me as well as comforts me. She is an encourager and I am grateful for her.

Lastly, one brother at my church is another one who I look up to in the spirit. Such wisdom that comes from him and he will challenge you to step out your comfort zone. He is one that doesn't just want you to hear him but wants what God has put in you to come out. He always reminds me that we serve the same God and that no person is better than the other. Just different. I praise God for all of these people I've named. Definitely grateful for them and who they are in my life.

Prayer for Chapter 6

Father, we come before you rejoicing. We thank you for everything you've done. We thank you right now for who you are. We thank you, Lord, that you have changed our hearts. Lord, we pray that we constantly seek you and never become complacent with you. We pray that the zeal of the knowledge of Christ eats us up and that we learn to love one another. Help us to never compromise who we are, no matter where we are or who we are around. Help us to keep our mind stayed on you, meditating on your Word day and night. These prayers do we ask in your precious holy name, Jesus, amen.

CHAPTER 6

Stay the Course

When you first find out who God created you to be, it can be a lot to process. It can be hard to believe. It sounds funny to say "you are meeting yourself," but when you have walked in other people's opinions as your own identity, you take on a certain belief system. Your potential will never surpass your belief system. Meeting the true you, though this is the real you, is a foreign belief system because you've never walked in it before. The process is for this reason, as we discussed in chapter 4. I named this chapter "Stay the Course" because not only do you have to take on another belief system for the true you, but others have to take on one as well. It can be tough because not everyone will accept the true you. The moment you start trying to walk in who you were created to be, there will be some tests and distractions to try to return you to what's familiar.

There are some people who don't recognize the potential within themselves. You can't discover your potential if you don't discover your true self. Once you understand who you are, you've pulled away from stereotypes and become an original. When you walk as an original, some might look at you and perceive you as arrogant or say things like "You think you're all that." The situations and circumstances you will face will give you thoughts like *Have I made a mistake? Am I wrong?* I'm not saying you shouldn't examine your character; you should. We want to stay in a place of humility and meekness. You are not wrong to examine the comment that was made to you. It could be God correcting you with the comment through that person. It's not easy, but I encourage you to keep moving forward.

Walking as an original brings strong confidence in who God says you are and surety within yourself that you now can no longer be moved by others' opinions. You don't have to seek validation from others, knowing God has already validated you. You are now set free from feeling like you have to compromise. Remain confident, but don't forget to be humble. There is a difference between being confident and being prideful. Your confidence is in God, not you. Confidence can hear correction; arrogance cannot. When you are a confident person, you can still learn, admit wrongs, and admit you don't know everything. When you are a prideful person, you cannot listen. A prideful person has a defense wall up for anyone who disagrees with them. They justify their wrongdoings. The prideful person takes time to grow, because it's hard to correct them.

It is important to be able to tell the difference because as you begin to see who God has called you, some of those names might come up from others. It can be discouraging, but you have to stay the course despite negative or misunderstood concepts of who you truly are. Remember, Jesus is your example, so examine yourself through him. With God, he'll give you discernment on who's supposed to walk with you. You may think certain people are supposed to be in your life, but they're not. You want to cut others out of your life, but you're not supposed to. There's a question that scripture asks that helps you determine God-ordained relationships. It says, "Do two walk together unless they agree to do so?" (Amos 3:3 NIV). Is the relationship agreeing with purpose, even if they are a Judas (traitor)? Is the relationship contradicting what God said in his Word?

Certain questions should be answered if it is truly a God-ordained relationship. There might be some people from the past who will not recognize who you've become but can only remember who you were. They might try to get you to walk back in the shoes of someone else or something else that isn't of God. Do not compromise. Stay steadfast on what God said about your life. If they can't walk with who God said you are, your true identity, often it can put us in a place where we're torn between two decisions. We should never compromise our identity in Christ. We can sometimes make the mistake of compromising our identity to make others happy. This will make us miserable because our peace is in our identity. If you decide to step out of your shoes, you step out of your peace to bring others peace. That should never be the case. There is always a cost for either direction you choose to go. If you stay steadfast on who God called you, persecution might come, and people might talk about you. If you leave your identity to be with others, you can be everyone's friend, but you won't feel right on the inside. It is your choice to make.

With this being said, though, don't assume before you encounter. This means don't think, *they will reject me or not like me* when it hasn't even happened yet. The biggest thing is not to compromise who you are. I made assumptions, thinking people wouldn't receive me before giving them a chance. Do not feel rejected, because you may not get rejected. The focus is to be you. God is steadily equipping you, and people are going to see that. Pray for them, point them to Jesus, give them keys, and encourage them to apply those keys to their lives, just like you did. Don't get upset if some people don't receive from you; maybe it's not their season to do so. It is possible that you're not even the one they're supposed to receive from.

While you are in this process of becoming, you want to walk with people who will help you stay on it and continue to become everything God has called you to be. An example of this in the Word is when Jesus was talking to his disciples: "'Be careful,' Jesus said of them, 'be on your guard against the yeast of the Pharisees and Sadducees'" (Matthew 16:6 NIV). He was talking about their teachings. The enemy doesn't want you to know who you are, because then you'll really realize the potential that you possess. You'll begin to walk in power and know what's in you. So the right influence still applies. The foundation of it should be Jesus Christ always. We need influences that are not contradicting what God has said. We are already being renewed in our minds and transformed from our old way of thinking daily, but certain things can trigger that old way of thinking again. Your influence always determines your direction. Whatever is influencing you is the direction you're going to end up.

The way you think is based off of your influences. We have to make sure it is the right voice, the right influence. There is a difference between good influences and right influences. We can often confuse these two, and it gets us off course. You begin doing a lot of good things, yet you are nowhere near where God wants you. Begin asking yourself, what is my purpose? What pleases God and what doesn't? What is my God-ordained assignment? These things help you determine your influence, which helps you stay the course. Staying on course is always bigger than you. When you stay on course, it will encourage others to do the same.

Jesus went through rejection, betrayal, and pain, yet he stayed the course. He is our Savior and also our example of how to stay the course during tests, trials, and life in general. It is bigger than us. Your potential is so massive that it can pave the way for others. There is nothing more peaceful and satisfying than to know who you are and to do what you were created to do. Some of you have kids. Set the example for them. There are teens reading this who have younger siblings and cousins looking up to them. Let's set the example by pointing them to Christ Jesus in speech and deeds. Don't give up, but keep striving forward, even if you might have doubters and discouragers while you are on the course. God has a promise, and the world has some opinions. What makes it hard is that it seems there are more opinions than anything. Allow God's voice, his calling on your life, to weigh more than people's opinions. Make it more valuable.

A scripture reads, "Let us not become weary in doing good for in the proper time we will reap a harvest if we do not give up" (Galatians 6:9 NIV). Keep going. Even when it gets hard, don't stop. See the goal. You and your mentor will work together to create in you a changed mentality. The Word also says, "Therefore, since we are surrounded around a great cloud of witnesses, let us throw off everything that hinders and the sin that so easily entangles. And let us run with perseverance the race marked out for us" (Hebrews 12:1 NIV). When things get hard for runners in track, their mentality is telling them, "Just a little further. You're almost there. Don't quit!" The process is not the prize. The prize is at the end of the process. You need to have a "why" to keep you focused through the process. Your why is what drives you, even when it gets hard.

Don't let hardship block your view of getting to the finish line. It's not easy; nothing really worthwhile that I know of is, but you can get there. If you can see it, believe that you can get it, stay committed, and chase it. We will walk in our true identity, we will fulfill our God ordained assignment, and we will live a life that is pleasing to God. The Lord has graced us to be victorious. Embrace the Word of God. Know that Jesus is with you and has overcome everything that is set to challenge you in life. Stay encouraged always. Let us all, as the Bible says, fight the good fight of faith. Remember that you are going forward for a purpose, but never forget what you have learned along the way. Some people do not know the potential that you are carrying. They don't know what God has put in you. Your purpose in life affects others. People are waiting for you to manifest what God has placed in you. God has put a key in you that can unlock something in someone else. In order to do this, you must not forget about your mat. We will discuss this more in the next chapter.

Testimony: Staying
the Course

A pastor once said a statement, and it encourages me even to this day. He said, "You cannot change what you're a part of." What he meant was how can I expect to affect the world when I am conforming to it? The process of you becoming who God has called you to be is bigger than you. I really had to zero in on this concept, because sometimes your past mentality can sweet talk you into missing it. When trying to walk with God, sometimes we can have those desires to do what we used to do, to be with the people God separated us from. When I really started understanding the Word of God, I wanted everybody to get it. Don't stop wanting that, but understand that when you go to share what God is doing in your life, or just sharing the gospel, you also can be walking into a test. Not everyone will get it, and you have to stay committed.

I would share the Word of God, but I would meet people who didn't really believe. Sometimes they were strangers, people I knew in past seasons of my life, and some were around when God began to change me. We can't let disagreements or unbelievers move our faith. I've run into people who only can relate to my past. I love them, but I also love God, and certain contradictions would arise at times. Things that I used to do or was okay being around began to contradict my relationship with Jesus. I was torn because I can choose to say no to them and risk losing my relationship with them, or I could go with them and do stuff I know God doesn't want and feel a conviction on the inside of me. Honestly, I've done both.

Not saying disobeying God is right; it's wrong, and I have learned from compromising at times. God would deal with me about it, and I knew I needed to change. Something I grew to know as the spirit dealt with me is that I don't have to compromise or bend even a little to get someone saved. The Bible says, "No one can come to me unless the Father who sent me draws them, and I will raise them up at the last day" (John 6:44 NIV). We don't draw them, the Father does. We are just the vessel God is using to spread the gospel. When we learn that, we don't have to compromise or think we have to change even a little to get someone saved. These are typical things believers face, and we have to stay the course and know that God is with us. You are not there to be self-righteous or mean to people in your disagreement with them, but always follow God over man. I had to learn that, and it was tough because of my people-pleasing background. This is to encourage you to stay the course. Always follow God. Still love people, but always follow God and stay planted in his Word.

Prayer for Chapter 7

Father, I thank you now for everything. As I continue my walk with you, keep me humble. Help me to be in a place where everything I do, I do it for the glory of you. Take away any spirit of pride and any prideful thoughts that try to come on me. Help me to walk in your will. In Jesus's name, amen.

CHAPTER 7

Don't Forget Your Mat

In the book of John, it says, "Then Jesus said to him, Get up! Pick up your mat and walk" (John 5:8 NIV). The mat represents a testimony. It represents tests and trials, mistakes made, false identities, all previous voids, and the wrong paths that you have taken trying to find your way. Do not think that any of it was for nothing. The Bible says, "And we know that in all things God works for the good of those who love him, who have been called according to his purpose" (Romans 8:28 NIV). Another scripture says "We glory in our sufferings, because we know our sufferings produces perseverance, perseverance produces character, and character produces hope (Romans 5:3–4 NIV). All of the things that you have been through have sculpted you into who God wanted you to be. I quoted the New International Version for Romans 5:3–4, but the King James Version talks about trials producing experience. You've developed a stronger character.

Your experience has produced counsel. The wisdom of God on the inside of you can help someone else.

All of your trials have produced a testimony, and the testimony is for someone else. The counsel you produce makes you a counselor for someone else who is dealing with the same thing you were seeking God about. Your mat gives God glory. Your mat encourages others in the Lord. Your mat keeps you humble because you remember where God brought you from. Now, before you go and share what God has done in your life, I want you to always remember this. The foundation of who you are as you walk in your identity should always be Jesus Christ. So your walk should always be in a place of love. I'm talking about the love that God has. Why? Because you have changed and been transformed to love on and help others. This includes those who have doubted and done you wrong. God doesn't do a work in us for revenge. It's not for us to go back to people in our past and say, "I told you I can do it," to rub it in their face. That's why the process and having a mentor is so important. You have to stay humble, knowing that everything you are, God did it, not you. We can't forget that. Don't get caught up in pride. The same God that elevated you and changed your life will humble you and bring you down if you try to walk in pride or try to take his glory.

It's important to praise God and give him the credit. It's great to seek the Lord in the pit. We pray, fast, and cry out to God to get out of the pit, but we can't forget God when we enter into the palace. The same God that was with you in the process when you were sad and were saying "help me" is the same God that brought comfort to you. Don't forget that. Now let us go and give him honor and glory. Go out and walk in love and confidence, spreading your testimony! Encourage your brothers and sisters in the Lord. Not just them, though, but also those who don't know God. Your testimony can reach the lost as well. One thing I believe is very important to share is how to love. When you discover who you are in Christ, you understand that you are created in God's image according to Genesis 1:26 (KJV). When you see that, you ask what does that have to do with love?

The Bible says, "And so we know and rely on the love God has for us. God is Love. Whoever lives in love lives in God, and God in them" (1 John 4:16 NIV). The scripture lets us know that God is love. So this lets us know that we are made in the image of love. Through your journey of discovering who you are, you'll begin to experience true love. No one can say they know love and don't know Jesus. Once you know the Lord, embrace true unconditional love, you'll finally be in that place to love yourself. Think about all of those standards you tried to live up to just to feel loved—having your hair styled a certain way, a huge house, luxury car, or stacks of money. Stop thinking you don't qualify to be loved just because someone didn't validate those things I listed. Stop allowing someone's opinions to determine your view about yourself. All of that thinking needs to change. Now, of course I'm not saying dress or look any kind of way, but when you know the Father's love, you will appreciate you. It will be real love and not a performance. You won't have to look for people to appreciate you, just to feel appreciated.

A lot of us struggled because our parents didn't validate us. It's time to experience the love from our Father in heaven. Let's experience his love, knowing that his validation toward us is the validation we need. You will know God's plan for your life and not try to compare your success to other people's. Relationships will change. I'm not saying compliments or advice are bad, but when who you are hangs on someone else's words and not God's, it's a problem. Love yourself, appreciate yourself, and remember that you can only give what's in you. How can you give love if you don't have love? Now, you may be in a place where you know yourself. Remember, there are others who need to discover themselves. Some people out there don't appreciate themselves because they don't know who they are. Some, because they don't know their identity in Christ, have even been tricked into believing lies, such as, they are not valued; no one loves them or cares for them. These lies were believed due to voids making room for them internally and not having the knowledge of Christ, which gave a place for the enemy to step in.

That's where we come in as disciples of Christ. We are here to spread the gospel. It's important for us to share the change in our hearts, the change in our lifestyle, and the change in our faith. We give God glory by walking in our identity, helping others build a true relationship with God through mentorship, encouragement, and most importantly loving them!

Testimony: Taking Up My Bed and Walking

My mat carries my childhood to where I am now. As the Lord lets me see more years, testimonies will continue to produce in my life so that more things can be written on my mat that I carry. As a kid, I didn't grow up in church. There are some who will pick up this book who also didn't grow up in church. Though I encourage church, I don't look down on you, and I pray God touches your heart to go now. We all need a church and a pastor. As a kid, I've had things spoken to me that were good and bad. People have said, "You have potential." Others' opinions toward me have been very discouraging. When I finally saw how good I became at working out, I cleaved to it. It was my ticket to gain recognition from others. Working out is great, but it is still external, so when I got diagnosed with multiple sclerosis, my ticket of recognition and acceptance was taken from me, in my eyes.

God wanted to show me something greater. He wanted to show me who I am. He wanted to show me I don't have to work extra hard in the gym to be accepted. The Bible says, "To the praise of the glory of his grace, wherein he hath made us accepted in the beloved" (Ephesians 1:6 KJV). I am already accepted in the beloved freely because of Jesus. So when I am not accepted by others, it's all right because Jesus has already accepted me. MS has made me legally blind, and my testimony is that it took me losing my natural vision to find out who I truly am. Nothing external defines me. I don't have to look for validation, because I'm already validated in Christ. I don't have to be sad or look down on myself and walk according to others' opinions anymore. I can walk in who I am in Christ.

Depression has hit me; suicidal thoughts have come, because I wouldn't accept my differences in fear of others not accepting them.

I'm thankful to say that because of Jesus Christ, I stand here changed. I would be one selfish person if I didn't share this with others. I am not the only one who had a hard time embracing his differences. Some people have spoken low of you, not knowing who you truly are. They have spoken low of your potential, causing you to believe them. I had to learn that no matter what opinions come our way— because someone will always have something to say, whether positive or negative—it doesn't define us. It is important to know that Christ Jesus and he alone defines us. My life is changed because of the Lord. What God has put in us is amazing and will manifest. You are blessed in Christ, you are wonderful, and you are loved.

To any teens reading this book, remember this: you are the future. What is poured into you is poured into the future. What you know is what the future knows. I pray you know the knowledge of Christ. I pray you guys make him your first love and hunger for him. I pray you guys are filled with the Holy Ghost. I don't believe you have to wait until you're grown to love Jesus or until a situation occurs to run to Jesus. Have him now. Know him now. Stay encouraged. I will continue to spread the gospel to everyone, and I pray you do the same. The Bible says, "Freely you have received; freely give" (Matthew 10:8 NIV). No matter what situations or circumstances I may have shared from my life, my goal is not to bring a perspective of division, anger, or revenge, but to have a godly perspective. I encourage everyone to walk in truth and the love of God. Confrontation and offense can happen, but continue to stand on the Word of God. Let us strive to be everything that God has commanded us to be. I love you all with the love of Jesus Christ!

Prayer

Father, I thank you now for your Word. I thank Jesus for being the way, the truth, and the life. Father, I pray that our eyes are filled with you, so that we may see how you see. I pray that we are able to see ourselves through the lenses of how you see us as well as other people. Help us, Lord, to see even you for who you truly are and not through the perspective of the world's misconception of you. Allow our eyes to be open in the spirit, so that we can fight our battles with our spiritual weapons. Give us the ability to expose any spirit of the enemy, since we know that we wrestle not against flesh and blood. I pray now that we stand strong on your Word and come against anything that contradicts it. We come into agreement with you, Lord, that we are everything you said we are. Give us discernment to know that anything or anyone who stands against you and your word is false. Let everything we do be for your glory. In Jesus's name, amen.

Printed in the United States
By Bookmasters